Fake Deep

by Jessica Universe

I would say none of this should be shared, but it's cool if you do. Just fucking credit me man. Don't be that popular poetry account who puts their watermark over other peoples' poems. Thanks man. Read responsibly, don't be a dick.

© 2017 by Jessica Universe LLC . All rights reserved.

love,
jessica
♡

# fake deep

to my momma

and my internet family

i don't want to call myself a poet

because i really have no idea what i'm doing

i don't want to call my shit poetry

because that seems like an insult to true poetry

but nevertheless

i hope you enjoy

i did

how are you gonna pretend

you experience life

more intensely

than someone else

just because you can

take prettier pictures

and use bigger words

literally

shut up

- *something i have to remind myself too*

*(i get it we all like sunsets & flowers)*

turns out

what makes you happy

(for the most part)

isn't where you are

it's who you're with

and that's a very sad realization for a lonely person

if we met at a different place in our lives

i think we would've hated each other

i'm glad we met the way we did

i can't imagine

not clinging onto every word you say

not getting flips and spins and butterflies

every time i see you

nor do i want to

some things

just really don't need to be said

if something is too good

or too perfect

you can't relate to it

it becomes untouchable

and then like what's the point?

basically that's what i'm telling myself

to comfort me on the fact that

i'm not a necessarily very poetic person

and you might be reading this like

"damn this is shitty"

but you understood it right?

and why read something you can't understand?

who are you

under your mental illness?

i don't care how much you're hurting

when everything is stripped away

the raw you

is why i'll stay

you know what you want

so do it

even if it's slowly

or however many other ways it could be less than ideal

it's a whole lot better than nothing

if that's where you were before

i know there is an obvious problem

with not finishing what you've started

but whether you even tried and failed

or just not tried at all

it's still not getting finished

and in the end

at least i spent all that time attempting something

even if i didn't accomplish it

instead of napping or some shit

something's gotta get you outta bed

sometimes life feels super clear

and i'm like yeah i do this and this will happen

then i'll be where i want to be

but most days

i'm sweaty and nervous and avoid thinking too hard

about anything

and i'll play guitar badly until my fingers ache

because everything is pretty scary

the only guaranteed thing about a person

is the promise they'll fuck up and let you down

eventually

you should know

it's not him making you feel wonderful

it's you letting yourself feel wonderful

because deep down you know

you deserve to be happy

but please be careful

if those wonderful moments are fleeting

and for the most part he makes you feel like shit

leave

i promise there are a million other people

that will make you feel wonderful

in a million other ways

i hope you find what makes you feel beautiful

and i hope it's more than just a person

capture all your moments

because everything happens so fast

and then it's over

i think for some reason

it's less scary

to have proof things happened

and proof you lived life

before it ends

isn't it terrifying

that us girls

have to choose

between expressing our disgust

or our life

because there's always that chance

the voice in our head

that wonders

if turning down that drink

or smacking away that hand

will get us killed

a man's ego

is a woman's killer

you are a long nap i didn't mean to take

great for the duration of the nap

but as soon as i'm completely awake

i feel like absolute shit, wasted my time,

and my mom is yelling at me

i feel like everything in life is give and take

once i almost got hit by a car while biking

later that night i was shaken up so bad that

i biked really slowly on a sidewalk to avoid cars

a guy walking past me decided to scream in my ear to

scare me off my bike

for fun

on the other hand

i always get amazing parking spots

and always get free extra fries

so maybe those annoying negative occurrences

are just upfront payments

for the good things that make your day

i'm sorry i promised you i'd stay

when i had no intention to

i guess i thought the hope you felt in the moment

would be worth the inevitable hurt you felt in the end

but after all the times people have

broken their promises to me

i know better now

sorry you were the last lesson

it took me before i learned

the best feeling is getting to finally pee

after holding it in for a while

i hope everyone meets a person

who makes you feel like that

when you pour your heart out to them

the whole hate towards the

"airhead pretty girl" trope

is a mess

because no girl is actually

empty

people are incapable of being

one dimensional

and

the fact we are deciding for someone else

if they are smart or interesting or deep enough

just proves we are all pieces of shit

who want to feel like we are better than others

we all have our biases

was it really what they did that upset you

or partially who they are

i would let my friends slide with a lot more shit

than i would let a stranger i just see online

and maybe we are forgetting

how absolutely

imperfect & hypocritical we all are

if you feel like you've plateaued

and things aren't getting much better

i think you should keep in mind

good things tend to happen all at once

change happens in clusters

why are you surprised?

humans will always grow tired

of not being treated like humans.

you say you love him

but why the fuck do you treat him like that?

you should know how much

things have changed since i met you

i didn't even realize a person

could be a favorite anything

but your voice is my favorite voice

your laugh is my favorite laugh

i wonder if there's even love after you

i don't even know if i want there to be

if you don't do it for yourself baby,

who will?

i'm beginning to suspect

when people can't

do something they want to do

they instead harass the people who are

capable of achieving it

the first thing i worry about is

if what i do hurts someone

i never really worry

if what they do hurts me

until i've already been hurt

you are given the choice to be anything

i can't believe some people choose to be hateful

the truest test of confidence

is how tall you walk

walking alone

straighten your back,

look up from the ground

you look incredible.

we all think we know shit

news flash

none of us know shit

and if you think you know shit

you should know you don't know shit

i want to experience love

specifically fall in love

and while i think love itself

is a conscious decision

dedication & hard effort

i think

there must be some kind of pull out there

undeniable attraction

to another human

i want to feel that

but i'm also so young

these damn romantic teen angst novels

got my hopes up for nothing

why am i nice?

well to be honest

i think you have to have a certain level of

disregard for others

to be mean

and i care far too much about people's

opinions

feelings

struggles

to allow myself to be unkind

also

i'm just a fuckin' pussy man

if i'm mean to someone

they have the right to be 10x meaner back

and i would

not

handle that well

no matter how many times

i've been hurt

i still see the best in people first

because there's seven billion of us

there's so many ways someone can be good

who am i not to give them a chance?

you don't need love

not like that

you don't need someone to hold

you don't need to be held

you don't need romance

i keep telling myself

marks

scars

scabs

give me character

but really

i just need to stop falling down

the fucking stairs

jesus christ jessica

we all live in different worlds

maybe our mistake is

assuming all our worlds are the same

i want to be open and honest about my mental illness

but still each time

i try to open up about it

i worry people will perceive my truth

as insecurity

as attention seeking

i guess the problem with a stigma is

it's engrained in us

even if we don't want it to be

color

color

color

did you think of the rainbow?

or did you think of the hues of humans?

i'm fine with caring too much

because can you imagine

how empty it must feel

to not care at all?

you don't have the right

to pick us apart

and take the best prettiest pieces

and discard the rest

you take us all

or you get nothing

- people of color

it seems

the quieter you are on your behalf

the more sure you are of your value

because why try to prove to others

what you know for yourself

if not out of fear

yes, you have a pretty face

but you and i both know

at any moment that can be taken away

i hope you find it in you

to be more than just pretty

i hope you find it in you

to be beautiful

kindness isn't a favor

i don't owe you anything

for your kindness

and you don't owe me anything

for mine

i get wanting a boy to like you

but you really don't have to

distance yourself from other girls

there's nothing wrong with being like other girls

if he's worth anything at all

he'll see how *you* you are

no comparisons

you don't need that

i don't know how you're feeling but

if it's bad i hope it passes

and if it's good i hope it lasts

why the hell do we normalize

boys having bad hygiene?

that's fucking gross

take a shower, wear deodorant,

clean under your nails

don't be nasty

it takes so little

to make my heart drop

but sometimes i forget

it might be that way for other people

so i apologize for shooting words like bullets

with no consideration for your heart

once i complained to my friend

that i hated how invested i was in

meaningless celebrity and internet drama

and how i didn't wan't to care

and he said

"okay, then don't care"

it changed my life

it's selfish of you to ask me to stay

can you not see how much you hurt me?

doesn't everyone deserve to feel beautiful in the one

and only vessel they can

live out their life in?

yet you're still telling me it's wrong to want girls that

look like me on the screens?

yet you're still silencing my desire to hear the story of

a girl who has lived like me?

yet you're still depriving me of shades

that my match my color?

what's up with that?

you try so hard to seem different

but everything you offer is the same

i have a tendency

to start things and never finish them

my theory is

i started life, but won't finish

making me immortal

i spend a lot of time not working

but none of that time really living

i don't do either of the things i want to be doing

that's the problem with being caught in the middle

what i'm saying is

please finish your tasks

so you can move on with more life

you know how when a cup is filled with

ice & water

when the ice melts the water doesn't overflow

there's probably an alternate universe

where everything is exactly the same

except when the ice melts

the water overflows

i guess i wanted to do my best to try and

make you feel the way i lived my life

but honestly

you can only understand me as much as

and the way

you understand yourself

i can't predict

how you would react to me

because i am me

and you are you

there's no way to separate

what i've experienced as

a female

an asian american

a teenager

i can't be one

without being them all

i know that

some people think

everything that has happened

becomes a little part of them

maybe that's true for you

but i don't think you have to

believe

anything you don't want to believe

and if you were hurt in a way

you did not want to let yourself be hurt

it's okay

to not let that

be something in you

if you do not want

to be weighed down

you don't have to be

we're all just a bunch of hypocrites and liars

trying to feel better because someone else is worse

why can a man be cruel but still loved

he's called raw & real & honest

i have never seen a cruel woman

who was still respected

a woman must always be kind

and soft and gentle and quiet

i'm not saying i like cruel people

but why aren't we, women, allowed to be?

if we wanted to?

i mean i'm assuming

who i am

is a collection of

the people i've met

the places i've been

the moments i've lived

the words i've read

the songs i've listened to

but honestly

i think i'm just a jumble

of bursts

of feelings

of sparks

and i don't think that's something

i could minimize

into tangible

words

sometimes i am so concerned

with how other people's minds work

i forget to wonder about my own

our entire lives are just repetitions of our habits

the most spontaneous thing you could do

is break a habit

nothing you are is something you have to be

i'd say i'm lost

but lost entails

i knew where i was going in the first place

which i don't

the people who don't like you

because you aren't like them

aren't people who need to like you anyways

i like how life sounds in poetry

a moment can be perfectly described with one

beautiful word

but in reality

the only words i can manage to tell you

are short and insignificant

many strung together

yet still

in no way can they summarize

the feelings i feel the way i feel them

what you liked in him

doesn't have to be what you like in me


what i liked in her

doesn't have to be what i like in you

even though

i don't know exactly who i am

right now

i feel very much myself in my body

when i think of just a few years before

i feel like a stranger to my past self

right now

i feel like i am me

but years from now

who will i be looking back at?

people only make remarks

about your health

and voice "concern" about your wellbeing

once it's visible to them

because who cares about anyone else

until it interferes with their life

recognizing that

people are shitty

and you are shitty

doesn't mean

you shouldn't try

to be

less shitty

be cautious with your heart and your trust

but never with your kindness

if you're a teen

and you think you're mature

or different

or have it figured it out

you're wrong lol

i am afraid of being toxic

because nobody will sit you down

and tell you

if you do this and it makes someone feel like this

it is wrong

and you should not do that

i don't think anybody has received

a crash course in

how to be the most uplifting

you can be

and we're all just trapped

in cycles of

slightly harming everyone we touch

which isn't much at first

until you've brushed souls

with hundreds of people

and your light isn't as bright as it used to be

and you don't know why

everyone you've ever held

got darker too

you were amazing

so slowly

i became you

and you became bored

because i don't think

you like yourself

the little bad things are the scariest

because they stack on top of each other

like tiny pebbles on the shore

and suddenly it's a dune

even the harshest waves can't break down

we let it get this big

we let it get this bad

and since nobody can pinpoint

one thing to topple the system over

here we are

trapped behind a mountain

of problems

that can't be named

and we wonder why we're drowning

you made me feel

like my favorite song

blasting with the windows down

and that's amazing

but i can't think straight

i can't act right

and how am i supposed

to love you

if i can only handle you

in small doses?

i understand why people hate labels

but i feel comfort

in being in a part of something

because everything else

feels kind of like a shot in the dark

and at least

i can be confused with people

just as confused the same way as me

is it unfair that

i like how you make me feel

but i loved him

for everything

he was

the way you move me

is with your words and promises

the way he moved me

was with his

everything

you don't truly know someone

until you've seen them angry

more specifically

angry

at you

i'm tired of hating myself

i'll be vain

i'm beautiful

i have a big heart

and a stunning mind

and i can make you laugh

and i deserve such good things

i love myself

i am a happy girl

obviously not all the time

i cry a lot you know

but

i like to be happy

more than i like to be sad

so i will call myself

a happy girl

because

that is what i am

happy

i scrolled back on my instagram

and i was smiling because i looked pretty

but i read through some of posts

and i saw the picture of the double rainbow

captioned

"when you see a double rainbow bc the universe is

telling you to stay"

and i forgot until i saw it

that was the last time i tried to kill myself

june 7, 2016

and i realize

how hard it is

to tell how someone is doing

i even forgot for myself

how miserable i used to be

because i was pretty

and i smiled

i am glad

i'm doing so much better now

you don't have to live their definition of success

you don't need a big house or a gucci belt

you can be content

with a pup and some CORN CHIPS

their success

doesn't have to be

your success

it has gotten so much better

it has gotten so much lighter

the dark isn't as dark as it used to be

i want to tell you to stay for the
sunlight
and the flowers in the spring
and the sound of laughter
and the taste of cinnamon
but
you should stay for you
you know
the you you'll meet
don't you want to meet yourself
when you are stronger
and happier?
i'm glad i got to meet myself today
i'm so different from me a few years
it's like i don't even know that me
who was she?
i'm doing much better now

one of our phases

will be our last phase

and then we fucking die

take all the fucking selfies you want

and post all the fucking selfies you want

life is too short and too difficult

not to revel in some vanity sometimes

why not scream to the world you're beautiful

we all die anyways

you broke my heart

but i expected it

so it's cool

didn't hurt any less though

life is so easy isn't it

you don't want to deal with something

so you say you forgot

you don't want to love someone anymore

so you say you never loved them in the first place

does everyone else live life without kindness?

"you should find someone you click with"

that's hard

"why would it be easy?"

*- conversation between my best friend and i*

how is she a downgrade

if she makes him happier

than you ever managed to?

there's kind people and nice people

you were neither

you're just a fuckin' dick lol

i wanted to show you my favorite

but i stopped

i turned off the song

i thought if i shared this with you

you would take it with you when you left

and i don't think i'm complete enough

to have pieces to spare

my mother is the

wisest

strongest

kindest

woman i know

and i feel sympathy for those

who never get to know her

like i know her

and i'm sorry for

people who aren't as close with

a parent

as i am with my mother

for it is

a blessing

i think the youth should be allowed

to make the silliest mistakes

but our generation

unfortunately

has everything we do documented and set in stone

online

and mistakes we should forget

will be remembered

because the CLOUD

backs up those screenshots

i don't know how to explain to you

any more than i already have

that people have colors

and some colors don't mix

and as much as i want to love you

i just don't think i can

i just don't think i should

because you can see her nipples through her shirt

every word coming out of her mouth

is bullshit

according to you

i mean i can't see your nipples

but you still sound stupid

what's your excuse?

you can adore yourself

you can fall in love with yourself every day

and still

have things you aren't entirely content with

that doesn't mean you deserve any less love

you can fix things about yourself

you can have a healthy relationship with yourself

without it being a perfect one

oh how i want to be loved

just

not

by you

i'm sorry to say

that life is not gentle

i want to be there

holding your hand

walking you through

but i can't

i'm not strong enough to carry us both

i have enough hardships on my own

and your problems

are not my problems

and i can't feel sorry

for finally putting myself first

*- a kind person turned terrible*

you made me feel guilty

for caring about myself

more than i cared for you

but you were with me for a moment

i'm with myself forever

i'm sorry for the way i made you feel

but i'm not sorry for choosing me

in this life

you must be selfish

keep your burdens light

keep your soul bright

i wrote all these love poems

with nobody in particular in mind

but i met you

and suddenly all of them

made sense

in a way i never expected

i don't know what i want

but i know it's not you

i'm beginning to think

every choice i've made

every mistake i've regretted

were all aligning a path

in this life

where i could meet you

and oh i'm so glad i did

i am dramatic

i live loudly

i talk loudly

i laugh loudly

i'm easily excitable

i'm emotional

i'm uncertain and impulsive

and i don't know why

you don't want me to love it

if i'm not who you thought i was

who did you expect me to be?

was it always like this?

some people you can talk to for months

and still feel like you don't know them

some people you can talk to a day

and somehow feel like

they were always meant to be in your life

me reacting to life: okay, cool

me reacting to life in poetry:

i screamed without words

because you were the sun

and who was i to darken your light

with my clouds

whether you hold back your heart

to avoid hurt

or give it everything you've got

you will still feel pain

it's unavoidable

so why live less

to hurt less

it's still gonna burn

but i'd rather feel a fire

we sure like to make fun of "cheesy" things

as if it's undesirable to express yourself

in a way everyone can understand

if live love laugh resonates with you

then live love laugh it all the way up

what's wrong with that?

you don't have to use a lot of words

to say a lot of things

i hope you don't think

now is as good as it gets

or at any point it can't get any better

because each part of your life

will have a different set of

happys and sads

and there is no one point where

everything is amazing

just moments of amazing

it's up to you

to be satisfied with that

my body is mine

my mind is mine

my soul is mine

my heart... not so much

in movies they cut out all the boring parts

and the good and bad happen all at once

but life as we live it

is mostly the boring, the buffer

and i'm still not sure

how to deal with that

please tell me why

pimples, breakouts, acne

are like the most common skin problem ever

but we all still feel like absolute shit

anytime we notice our skin is freaking out a bit

myself included

i literally cancel plans

because my forehead isn't as smooth

as i want it to be

i wish i could be able to tell you right now

that skin imperfections don't matter

but they still matter to me

and i have no business giving advice

i can't take

so what i'm asking you is

can we figure this out together?

so we can all feel a little less ugly?

i'm sixteen

i think i'm a whole lot more grown

than i really am

so i assumed i needed to wait

two years

until i'm eighteen

to do what i really want

but there is no later

because if tomorrow never comes

today was your last later

and you really can't stall

can you?

the cruelest thing about me is

i will never let you matter more in my life

than i matter in my life

maybe our moments were special

but once you're gone

you can't be special to me anymore

my life is my own

i won't let you be a part of it

it's a self preservation thing

not personal

oh love,

you complain they keep

taking from you

but you're giving them

so much to take

don't trust

the girl with words like sugar

or the boy with lips like honey

they will smother you

in the most golden gold

you might ever see

but if they leave

no one else's color

will look quite the same

will it

understand

that intentions don't matter

your soul could be yearning

to cover me in light

and love and softness

but if your actions suffocate me

in cold, in darkness, in despair

i'm still the one in pain

i feel incomplete

but i know the more i live

the more me there will be

so don't you dare

look me in the eyes

and promise

you're a piece

of a puzzle

i need

for the people

who have scrubbed their skin raw

in the shower

brushed their teeth

until their gums bled

and threw away the toothbrush

i'm sorry for how alone you feel

i'm sorry for how guilty you feel

i wish i had lived a life of experience

of healing to share

but i haven't

all i can offer is

you're not alone

you're not alone

you're not alone

you are clean.

on behalf of the kids

who have a beautiful mind

but no voice to speak it

but no art form to project it

i'm sorry we might never be able to hear

those lovely thoughts of yours

and see the brilliant images

your mind is begging to offer

i hope you find a way

i think i'm terrified

because i never let someone matter

so much to me

that i can't imagine coping if they left

but when i think of

you leaving

my heart stops

so do my lungs

i would always picture the end

with everyone i've met

just to prepare

but i can't see an end with  you

i have never wanted forever with someone

the way i want forever with you

it's terrifying

hurt is black and white

happiness is colors

i understand why it's so hard

to stop your eyes

from wandering back to him

when he has so much

blues and reds and rainbows to offer

it's almost like you

can't see the grey

i'm never worried

about running out of words

because i think of you

your smile

your laugh

your voice

and i find every word

i'll ever need

i thought i'd always be the one

writing love poems for nobody

pretending my heart was in the clouds

when it was with me on the ground

but something about you

makes every word come true

i'm guilty

i tell everyone to create their own joy

when i was in my shit

pulling storm clouds over me like a hoodie

i met you

and the rain cleared

and i hear the birds sing

and i feel the sunlight glaze my skin

i never thought happiness

could happen like this

i was so used to doing it alone

but maybe it's good to not be lonely

maybe you can't pluck out

the bad things in you

but you can fill yourself up

with so so much good

there's almost no room for the bad

you might miss high school or

you might look back and shudder

either way it's temporary

either way try to make the best of it

even if it sucks

it passes

english wasn't my first language

the kids at school bullied me for it

so i learned english and never looked back

now my korean is jumbled

i can't read it

i can't write it

i just hope you know

you don't have to be

whiter than you are

to fit into this western world

you don't have to bleach your skin

or stop eating your mom's cooking

you don't have to shy away

from saying certain words

because you don't say them "right"

you can be bold with the color in your blood

you can be angry and loud and passionate

you can be colorful

color is not dirty

you couldn't have been made more perfect

even if i plucked an angel from the sky

and asked them to sculpt you

from stardust and sugar and sunlight

don't doubt that

people expect more from kind people

people always want more kindness

over cruelty

nobody begs a cruel person to be cruel

it's scary before it happens

because you don't know what to expect

but once it's over it feels fine

doesn't it?

so jump

i know i can be happy without you

but it's a different kind of happy

and i want the kind of happy

we have now

the level of happiness i feel nowadays

is happier than i've ever felt in the past

it's crazy, i feel like light is bursting from my chest

i feel like happiness is oozing out

and i can't stop smiling

i hope everyone has felt this type of happy

i hope everyone eventually does

please don't doubt yourself

you are a cup of steamy matcha tea

why are you hurting over someone

searching for a soda pop

you can't be what they might want

you don't have to be

someone is searching for a you

don't change

i tell myself that

maybe the only things i share

the only words i say

should hold depth and weight

but you know

i like talking

about all the little things

and maybe what doesn't matter to me

slips off my lips

and really makes someone happy

is that silly?

if i can make someone laugh

i think that's a conversation with value

i fall really hard

really fast

i'm intense

i burn too hot

too bright

but you know what

i'm going to keep living like this

until i can't anymore

you can leave him

you don't need him

nobody is trying to hurt you

everybody is just trying

not to get hurt themselves

it can just be difficult

being on the receiving end

of selfishness

being happy is deciding

a compliment means more

than you might shrug it off as

that the weather is

not just okay but perfect

that a problem isn't a barricade

but a hurdle

being happy is realizing

maybe your mental illness

can make it harder

but it's worth all the effort

i'm sorry if seeing this

makes your hands shake

and your breathing uneven

but you can't lay around

expecting to figure it all out

in the silence of isolation

you have to hurt and yell and cry

you have to go out and live

you have to make mistakes

you have to get in trouble

if you want to live the type of life

people write chronicles about

you can't just be

the one who reads them

but if you're comfortable

with the quiet

you can lay back down

all i'm asking

is for you to decide

please think for yourself

no matter how sweet

their vanilla scented words may smell

don't forget the butter

and flour and salt

you can't bake the whole cake

with what little they give you

i think i'm using a cake metaphor

because i'm hungry

but what i'm trying to say is

think for yourself

for real

sometimes being told

something you already know

sounds different

with a different tone

from a different person

at a different volume

i hope you hear

you're beautiful

a million times

a million ways

from a million people

until you finally find

the one that clicks

and i hope even more

that voice is yours

when i am depressed

i forget how it felt to be happy

i feel empty, lost, and utterly alone

i feel cold and distant

like i'm watching my life

on a black and white television

ten feet away in a dark room

oh, but when i'm happy

the world sure does beam and gleam and glow

i feel light and bright and silken

i smell roses and nutmeg and caramel

i can't believe i used to want to stop it all

just to stop the sad

when there's so many ways my days can be great

even if not everyday

it's a price that's worth to be paid

every word they spit

that cracks a piece inside you

collects rubble in your soul

you could let it sit there

you could let yourself stay shattered

or you can take every shard of you

and build a suit of armor and a castle

you could build a library and a rose garden

you can do whatever you want with yourself

you are yours

despite what's been done to you by others

passion won't last forever

the spark starts the fire

but discipline and dedication

is what you need to keep it burning

the quickest route to self love

is deciding right now you respect yourself

that you hold value and meaning

and that in no way are you better or special

compared to anyone else

because what makes you worth loving

isn't that you are more than someone

but rather if you can love others

despite their flaws and mistakes

you can love yourself

even when i've poured my heart out

over 100 pages

i still feel

there's so much more left to be said

so much more

and that's how it's always going to be

talk a million miles a minute

for hours

and still feel there's words

forever trapped in your head

thank you.